Careers

371.425

People at Work
Creative
and Media

Jan Champney *Photographs by* Chris Fairclough

FRANKLIN WATTS
LONDON•SYDNEY

For Emma

First published in 2008 by Franklin Watts
338 Euston Road, London NW1 3BH

Franklin Watts Australia
Level 17/207 Kent Street
Sydney NSW 2000

Copyright © Franklin Watts 2008

Editor: Julia Bird
Art Director: Jonathan Hair
Designer: Jane Hawkins
Photography: Chris Fairclough (unless otherwise credited)

Picture credits:
p.12: the Advertising Archive; p.24: istockphoto © Peter Finnie; p.25: (top) Shutterstock © Galina Barskaya; p.28: (top) © the Royal Philharmonic Orchestra.

Every attempt has been made to clear copyright. Should there be any inadvertent omission please apply to the publisher for rectification.

A CIP catalogue record for this book
is available from the British Library

ISBN: 978 0 7496 7823 4

Dewey Classification: 302.23

Printed in China

Franklin Watts is a division of Hachette Children's Books,
an Hachette Livre UK company.
www.hachettelivre.co.uk

Note to parents and teachers: Every effort has been made by the Publishers to ensure that the websites on p.31 of this book are suitable for children, that they are of the highest educational value, and that they contain no inappropriate or offensive material. However, because of the nature of the Internet, it is impossible to guarantee that the contents of these sites will not be altered. We strongly advise that Internet access is supervised by a responsible adult.

Contents

Creative and media

Do you enjoy writing, drawing or performing? Have you thought about working in the **creative and media** sector?

There are lots of different jobs on offer but it can be a competitive world to enter. You will need excellent skills, talent, hard work and sometimes a bit of luck.

Photographers work in the creative and media sector.

Jewellerymakers need an artistic eye in their work.

Radio presenters often help to write and research their own shows.

First of all, it helps to know about the variety of jobs on offer in the creative and media sector. They can be divided up into four main groups:

- writing and **publishing**
- art and design
- creative and craft
- stage and performance.

Dancers have to work very hard to achieve their dreams.

Key Questions

Why do you think creative and media can be a competitive sector to work in?

What do you think might be the good parts of working in the creative and media industry?

Book publishing

The publishing industry in Britain employs nearly 300,000 people. Books, newspapers, **journals** and magazines are all produced by publishing companies.

There are two main types of book publishing, fiction and non-fiction. Fiction books involve stories that come from the author's imagination and are not based on fact. Non-fiction publications are based on real events and facts. Non-fiction books include dictionaries, biographies and educational books.

Anne writes fiction for children.

Anne says:
"I write stories for children and teenagers. I usually start off with an idea like what would happen if an alien rocket ship crash-landed on Earth? This starts off a story. Then I ask myself the question what happens next? I type my story onto a computer. When it's finished I print out a copy and send it to my publisher. An artist has to design a really good cover. Then the books are sent to the shops for people to buy."

Books are stored in huge warehouses before being sent out to bookshops and libraries.

Between **commissioning** or writing a book and publication, there are several stages of editing and production. The people working in publishing houses have to make sure each stage is followed and that each new book will sell.

Here are the main job areas in book publishing:

Editorial Commission and edit the book and look after its progress.

Picture research Find photographs for the book from picture libraries and photographers.

Production Work with the **reprographic house** and printer to get books completed on time.

Design Responsible for the book's overall 'look'.

Marketing Make sure that the books are **advertised** and sold into the right places.

Sales Sell the books into shops, school and library suppliers and other outlets.

Rights Negotiate with other companies for the ability to publish the book in different languages in other countries.

Most departments have assistants and this can be a good starting point for learning about the industry.

Sandra is an editorial assistant.

Sandra says:
"I help the editors with **proof-reading** and I sometimes help find pictures for the books. I also keep in touch with the authors. I'm learning a lot from my job and one day I'd like to be a commissioning editor."

Newspapers and magazines

The work of publishing books, newspapers and magazines is very similar. The main difference is that the **deadlines** for producing newspapers and magazines are tighter than those for books.

Newspaper writers, called journalists, and editors can often have just a few hours to get an important story or article into print, so there can be a lot of pressure in their work.

Peter is a journalist for a local daily newspaper. He says:

"I started working for a small newspaper as a trainee journalist. At first I got all the boring jobs, but now I've got more experience I'm given some great stories to follow. It can be very exciting reporting on something that will be important to our readers. I spend some time writing up the stories in the office and the rest I'm out interviewing and talking to people."

Good computer skills are very useful if you are interested in becoming a journalist.

Magazines are usually published weekly or monthly, so deadlines are more relaxed than in newspaper publishing. However, magazine staff have to be used to working ahead of schedule and responding to last-minute events.

Poppy is the editor of a snowboarding magazine. Poppy says:
"My main duties are choosing the stories for the magazine, picking the cover image and writing **cover lines**. We have to be good at keeping up with the **market** and making sure that our articles stay relevant and interesting for our readers."

Key Questions

What do you think are the main differences between newspaper and magazine journalism?

What skills does a good journalist need to have?

A magazine editorial team talk over new ideas for the magazine.

Broadcast journalism

Not all kinds of media involve printed publications. Broadcast journalists also write for television, the radio and for internet websites.

Like newspaper and magazine journalists, broadcast journalists find and follow up news stories and conduct interviews. However, they also need to think about the best way to present their story, especially if it is going to be seen on television.

Emily is training to be a television journalist. She explains:
"I've always wanted to be a journalist and am training to be one with a course in broadcast journalism. The hours can be long and a bit unpredictable if you're following up a big story, and you often have to work at weekends. But I like getting out and about and I get a real buzz when my stories get picked to be on the news."

Radio presenters need to have some technical knowledge of how radio broadcasting works.

Broadcast journalism can be a competitive world to enter, so it helps to get any work experience you can.

Internet journalism

The growth of the internet has meant that more and more people every year are becoming internet journalists. Their stories, articles and **blogs** are published online for people to read. Some internet journalists may have special training in **web design** to help them in their work.

Danny presents a radio show for a local station. He says:

"I started off by working as a trainee broadcast assistant at a local station. First of all I worked on late-night shows. It's hard working at night but it's all good experience. You have to be able to think on your feet in this job so that you can fill the silence if anything goes wrong. A good speaking voice is also a real must!"

The world of advertising

Any kind of publishing relies on **advertising**. In today's world, we are surrounded by advertising. When we turn on the television or radio or pick up a magazine, adverts jump out at us.

 iPod

Creating a poster like this involved an advertising team of people, including a director, photographer and designer.

Advertising teams include advertising executives and assistants who work together to create different **advertising campaigns**. These campaigns are designed to make us buy a particular **product** or **service**.

Andy is an advertising account executive.

"To work in advertising, it helps if you are creative and are an ideas person. You must also be able to work in a team and be good at communicating with your **clients**. Although many people enter advertising with **qualifications**, I started as an advertising assistant and have worked my way up through the company. If I can do it, so can you."

An advertising campaign is discussed with **clients**.

Key Questions

Which advertising campaigns do you remember?

Why do you think that is?

Can you think of five different advertising slogans or 'catch phrases'?

Photography

Photography is very important in the creative and media industry. Good photographs can bring non-fiction books, news reports and advertising campaigns to life.

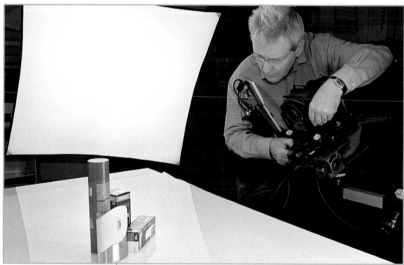

Tim is a **freelance** photographer. He takes photographs at weddings and other events, as well as family portraits. He works both in a **studio** and out **on location**.

Tim sets up a photo shoot in his studio.

Tim says:
"I love my job. When I first left school I worked in an office and photography was just a hobby. One day, my friends asked me to take their wedding photos. They turned out so well I was asked to do another. Eventually I decided to train as a photographer and I'm still at it, ten years later!"

Many photographers specialise in particular areas of photography, such as news, fashion or sport. Russell is a press photographer for a local newspaper.

? Key Questions

What do you think would be the good and bad aspects of being a photographer?

Do you think photographers should be allowed to take any photos they like for the sake of a good story?

Photographers often hire assistants to help their shoots go smoothly. Assistants can help with looking after clients, hiring locations, finding props and processing images.

Press photographers like Russell have to be used to carrying heavy equipment.

Artist and illustrator

Some people are lucky enough to turn their interests or hobbies into a career. If your talents lie in painting or drawing, a career as an artist or illustrator could be for you.

Making a career out of being an artist or illustrator can be difficult. It takes hard work, determination and, of course, a bit of luck.

Neal is an artist.
"I've always painted and drawn. When I left school, I decided to go to art college. I learned about different styles of art and how to use different art **materials**, such as paint, ink and crayon. The work isn't always steady and so my earnings can go up and down, but I'm lucky because I get to do what I love every day."

Artist Neal adds the finishing touches to a painting of a snowy landscape.

An illustrator is a particular type of artist. Illustrators specialise in doing drawings for books, magazines, comics and greeting cards. Some illustrators work by hand, while others use computers to create their drawings.

Annette at work in her studio, illustrating a children's book.

Annette is an illustrator. She says:
"My studio is the room that used to be our spare bedroom! I use my drawing board, computer and paints to design and create my work. I design book covers and illustrate the pages of books and magazines. To be a good illustrator you need a good imagination and drawing skills, so my advice to anyone wanting to do this job is to just keep practising!"

Key Questions

Name some famous artists and illustrators that you have heard of. What makes their work stand out for you?

Sculptor and jewellery designer

Sculptors are artists, too. They use different types of materials such as clay, metal and wood to create sculptures.

Patrick is a sculptor. He says:
"The materials I use depend on the size of the work and the type of sculpture I'm designing. If it's very big I like using strong materials, such as iron or steel. If it's smaller, I use clay or even paper. I've had to learn lots of different skills in my work, such as cutting and joining metal or **firing** clay. Sometimes I think up and design the sculptures myself. At other times, the customers design the sculptures and I make them."

Famous sculptors
There have been some famous and talented sculptors. See if you can find out more about Henry Moore, Barbara Hepworth and Auguste Rodin.

Like sculptors, jewellery designers use different materials in their work. Designing and making jewellery takes a lot of skill. Cutting, bending and heating different metals such as gold and silver needs plenty of practice.

Jon says:
"I design, make and sell jewellery. When I was at school I sold earrings and bracelets to my friends, but I didn't think jewellery could be my career until I started a jewellery course. I learned lots about different materials and my teachers gave me advice about how to set up a business. I now sell my jewellery at craft fairs and on my own website."

? Key Questions

What materials can sculptures be made from?

What materials can jewellery be made of?

Jon displays some of the jewellery he has made.

Fashion and interior designer

If your dream is to design and create clothes, be warned - the fashion industry is very competitive.

A fashion designer needs an eye for fashion and strong knowledge of design. He or she must also be prepared for lots of hard work!

Anne is a fashion designer.

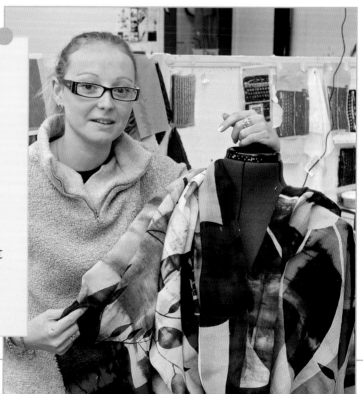

Anne says:
"When I finished school I went to art school for three years. Then I did a two-year college course in fashion and **textiles**. The course was great fun, but really hard work. I'm now getting some work experience with a high-street fashion designer. I'm hoping that it will give me the edge when I start applying for jobs."

Interior designers use fabric in their work.

Interior designers use their skills to design and furnish a variety of places, including homes, offices, shops, hotels and restaurants.

Janette is an interior designer.
"When I left school I didn't know what I wanted to do, so I worked in a supermarket. One day, I decided to redecorate my living room. My friends were really impressed with the results so I helped them to do their houses too. One of them suggested I should train as an interior designer. Fifteen years later I'm still doing it and the business is doing well!"

Key Questions

Why do you think fashion design is so competitive?

How would you choose to decorate your bedroom?

Performing

The performance industry makes up an important part of the creative sector.

There are lots of job opportunities in the performance industry, which includes television, radio, theatre, dance and musical performance. Some jobs require lots of qualifications while others need very few.

Generally, in television and on the stage, the jobs can be divided into 'on stage' and 'off stage'. 'On stage' describes the dancers, singers, actors and other performers. 'Off stage' describes the people who work with sound, lighting, cameras, make-up, costumes and scenery.

Both on- and off-stage workers need to work together to ensure a film production is a success.

Actors are the face of any production. Acting is one of the most difficult and competitive careers to enter, and any training you can receive helps. Successful actors can work in television, film, the theatre and radio.

Orele is an actor. He says:
"I've been an actor for five years. I went to drama school to learn as much as I could. Over the years I have had to do some funny jobs, including being a chicken in an advert! At other times, I've worked in a bar to pay the rent. Sometimes it can be hard to keep going but it's all worth it when I'm working."

Orele in pantomime costume.

Key Questions

Have you ever been to the theatre? What did you enjoy about it?

What do you think are the difficult parts of being an actor?

Script writers
Plays, films and television programmes have **scripts** that are written by script writers. Script writers have to research the characters they are including and make sure every fact is accurate. When the actors start reading the script, the writer often has to change things. Authors, journalists and actors have all become script writers.

Dancers and choreographers

Dancers perform in all sorts of productions, including ballets, musicals and music videos.

Dancers usually have to work hard from a young age to follow their dream. To stay fit, dancers need to eat sensibly and look after their bodies very carefully. A bad injury can wreck a promising dancing career.

John is a jazz dancer. He says: "I was six when I started dancing. I got bullied for it when I was little but I didn't care because I knew that one day I would become a **professional** dancer. I was very proud to win a place at a dance school as there was a lot of competition. My first **auditions** didn't work out, but I kept trying and eventually I got a job dancing in a show. You can't give up if you want to dance!"

Ballet
Ballet dancers usually begin lessons at a very young age, often as young as four or five. The most talented ballet dancers will go on to study at a special school where they have ballet lessons every day, along with normal lessons. The most famous ballet school in the UK is the Royal Ballet School in London.

A **choreographer** is very important to a dance company. They work with the dancers, helping them to choose which steps to perform to the music and in what order.

Every dance performance is very carefully choreographed.

Jane is a modern dance choreographer.
She explains what makes a successful choreographer:
"It's important to love dance, music and all types of performance. But it's also important to want to tell the audience a story. Good dancing can make an audience sad, happy and even scared. It's all about understanding and loving dance and knowing how the body moves."

Key Questions

Why do you think dancers start learning to dance at a young age?

Can you name any other jobs where taking good care of your body is important?

The backstage team

Any TV, film or theatre production needs a strong **production team**. There are a variety of jobs in production.

A producer heads the production team and looks after a performance from start to finish. A producer helps to raise funds to allow the performance to take place and will have the final say on the production. Producers are helped by production assistants.

Sally-Anne is a production assistant on a TV show. "I was studying journalism before I applied for my first job as a research assistant for a TV show. It can be hard work as you spend a lot of time away from home shooting on location, and the hours are long. But the work is varied and can be great fun."

The director's chair
Every production also needs a director. A director decides things like camera angles, the way actors say their lines and what a set should look like. Some directors have a qualification in directing but many others have worked their way up through the industry. Famous directors include Stephen Spielberg and Alfred Hitchcock.

Runner

A runner is often a first job in TV, radio or film. To be a runner you don't need any qualifications but you do need a strong interest in the industry. You'll also have to work hard. The tasks a runner might do on a shoot include hiring props, helping to set up a shoot, answering the phone and looking after the **cast**.

Camera operators work with digital, electronic or film cameras to shoot pictures or videos. Some have taken a television or film course, but others work their way up from being camera operator's assistant.

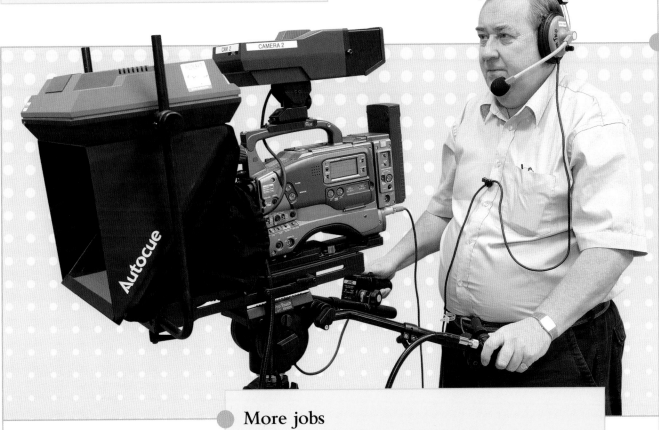

It takes a lot of skill to operate video camera equipment well.

More jobs

There are a variety of other jobs in TV, theatre and film, many of which you can start as an assistant and learn more on the job. These include jobs in:

- Costume design
- Set design and construction
- Lighting and sound.

Musician

Have you ever thought about becoming a professional musician?

A symphony orchestra performing.

There are lots of musical styles such as classical, pop, rock, jazz and folk. Some musicians play music that they've written. Others, such as orchestra or band musicians, perform music that has been written by other people.

Katie is a professional violinist. "I've always known that playing the violin was what I wanted to do as a career. I passed my Grade 8 exams and auditioned for a local orchestra. I got accepted and have worked there ever since! We practise every afternoon and perform most evenings. When we are **touring** I can be away from home for several months and miss my family. Although it's hard work I'm happy to be paid for doing what I enjoy."

Dave sings and plays the guitar in a band. The band performs songs they have written, as well as some songs by other bands, known as covers.

Dave says:
"Music is a real passion for me. I started playing the guitar when I was a kid, and later on I discovered a talent for writing my own songs. My band plays a mixture of rock and pop music. We perform at special occasions, such as parties and weddings, and travel all over the country to play. It's great to get people dancing and singing along!"

Dave and his band enjoy performing to a crowd.

Behind the scenes
Like TV, film and theatre performers, musicians need a strong production team. Jobs in the industry include music producers, **recording engineers** and stage crew for live performances.

Key Questions

Apart from musical talent, what skills do you think a member of an orchestra needs?

What about a singer in a band?

Glossary

Advertising Using the media, such as TV or the internet, to sell a product or service.

Advertising campaigns Packages of advertising designed to sell something.

Audition A trial performance by an actor, dancer or musician to get a part in a production.

Blog A diary of someone's thoughts, opinions and experiences that is posted on the internet for others to read.

Cast All the actors in a play, film or television production.

Choreographer Someone who puts dance steps together for a performance.

Clients Customers.

Commissioning Making an agreement to produce something.

Cover lines The words on the front of a magazine or newspaper that introduce the stories that it contains.

Creative and media The family of jobs in the arts and media, including television, radio, music and film.

Deadline Time limit.

Firing The process that heats clay.

Freelance Someone who works for his or herself, rather than for a company.

Journals Publications about particular subjects, for example medicine.

Market The customers for a particular product or service.

Materials The substances or things that an object is made of.

On location Film or photographic work that is done away from the studio in a particular setting, often outside.

Product Something we buy.

Production team The people who work behind the scenes to produce something, for example a song or a TV show.

Professional Someone who is paid to do a job.

Proofreading Checking written material for mistakes.

Publishing Producing printed material, such as books, newspapers and magazines.

Qualifications Something, such as a degree or a diploma, which proves you have studied a subject to a certain level.

Recording engineer Someone who oversees music being recorded in a studio.

Reprographic house A place where pages are prepared for the printer.

Research To find out as much as possible about a topic, person or event.

Script The written version or text of a performance.

Service Work done for others.

Studio A room where an artist, musician or dancer works.

Textiles Fabric or cloth.

Touring Performing in a number of different places.

Web design Designing web pages for the internet.

Skills and Training

You now know that the creative and media industry has lots of different jobs on offer.

Many need special skills and training. You can develop these skills by going to college or university. However, there are other jobs that can be done with only a small amount of training.

Training and Qualifications table

Commissioning editor Editor Newspaper writer Newspaper editor Journalist Advertising account executive	Degree/and or high level of experience
Dancer Artist Illustrator Sculptor Fashion designer Interior designer Script writer Photographer Choreographer Film producer Director Radio presenter Musician	High level of talent and/or experience. Many may also have a degree
Publishing assistant Author	2-3 A-levels NVQ Level 3 Level 3 diploma
Camera operator Production assistant	Few or no qualifications

The ladder shows the usual qualifications normally needed for each job. The qualifications you can take will depend on what is on offer in your area. Many people working in the Creative and Media sector have as much talent and determination as they do qualifications.

If you want any advice, ask your careers teacher or Connexions PA.

Advertising Association
020 7340 1100
www.adassoc.org.uk

Arts Council of England
0845 300 6200
www.artscouncil.org.uk

Association of Illustrators
020 7613 4328
www.theaoi.com

Association of Photographers
020 7739 6669
www.the-aop.org

Design Council
020 7420 5200
www.designcouncil.org.uk

National Council for the Training of Journalists
01299 544014
www.nctj.com

Publishing Association
020 7691 9191
www.publishers.org.uk

Scottish Arts Council
0845 603 6000
www.scottisharts.org.uk

SkillFast-UK (Sector Skills Council for fashion and textiles)
0113 239 9600
www.skillfast-uk.org

Skillset (Sector Skills Council for the audio visual industries)
08080 300900
www.skillset.org

Society of Authors
020 7373 6642
www.societyofauthors.net

Index